Practical C++ for Beginners

A concise and friendly introduction to programming

First Edition

Practical C++ for Beginners

A concise and friendly introduction to programming

Okwu C. Daniel

Page left blank intentionally

Preface

This book is an introduction to C++ and programming; it teaches the fundamentals of computer programming in general. Whilst those with prior programming knowledge can benefit from this book, no prior programming experience is required. It is suitable for secondary school students, undergraduates and beginners in programming. Experienced programmers who want to learn C++ will find the book useful.

Many examples are used to demonstrate how to apply programming concepts. It is recommended that readers type these examples and run the programs.

Consistent practice is important for learning how to code. It builds up confidence and allows programming principles to be seared into one's mind. There are exercises at the end of each chapter for practice and reinforcement of the concepts taught.

Whilst the book is not encyclopedic in content, over-simplifications are avoided; it contains the essentials of programming and coding in C++.

Page intentionally left blank

Table of Contents

About the Author

Okwu C. Dan has degrees in Computer Science. He holds certifications from The Computing Technology Industry Association (CompTIA) and Microsoft. His areas of interest include computer programming, computer networking, relational database and teaching. He blogs at https://bytevista.com/blog.

Page intentionally left blank

Chapter 1: Introduction

Objectives

- Define programming,
- Set up your programming environment,
- Write a C++ statement and execute it.

1.1 What is programming?

Programming is the act of writing instructions for a computer. The instructions are written in a particular computer language. The instructions are usually written using English and mathematical notations (high-level language). Given that computers understand only instructions expressed as 0s and 1s (machine language), they must be translated using a compiler or interpreter.

The set of rules that guides how instructions are written for a computer in a particular language is known as syntax. The instructions for a computer must be unambiguous and syntactically correct.

Why you should learn C++

C++ is a versatile high-level language. Although C++ is an old programming language, it is a popular language that is used in Arduino boards, cars, aircrafts, robots and in creating games, desktop and mobile applications. C++ is a popular and fast robotic programming language.

1.2 Set up your programming environment

Visit https://www.fosshub.com/Code-Blocks.html?dwl=codeblocks-20.03mingw-setup.exe to download Code::Blocks

Installing Code::Blocks

i. Click the installer and follow the prompts which require you to click Next, I Agree and Install.

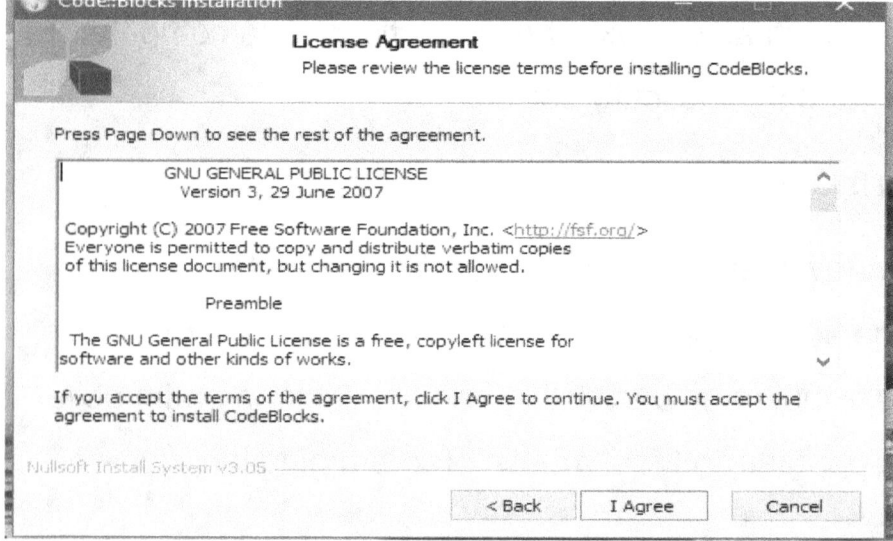

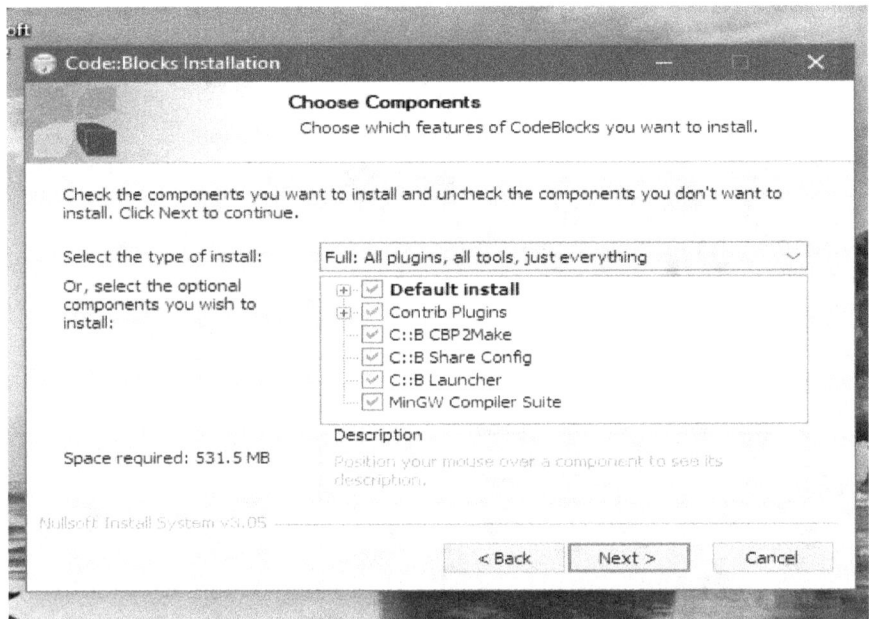

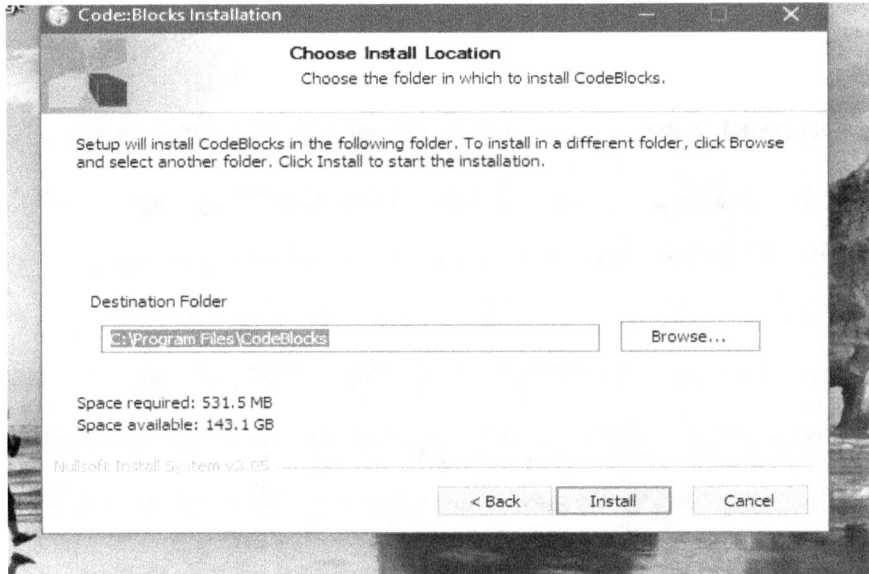

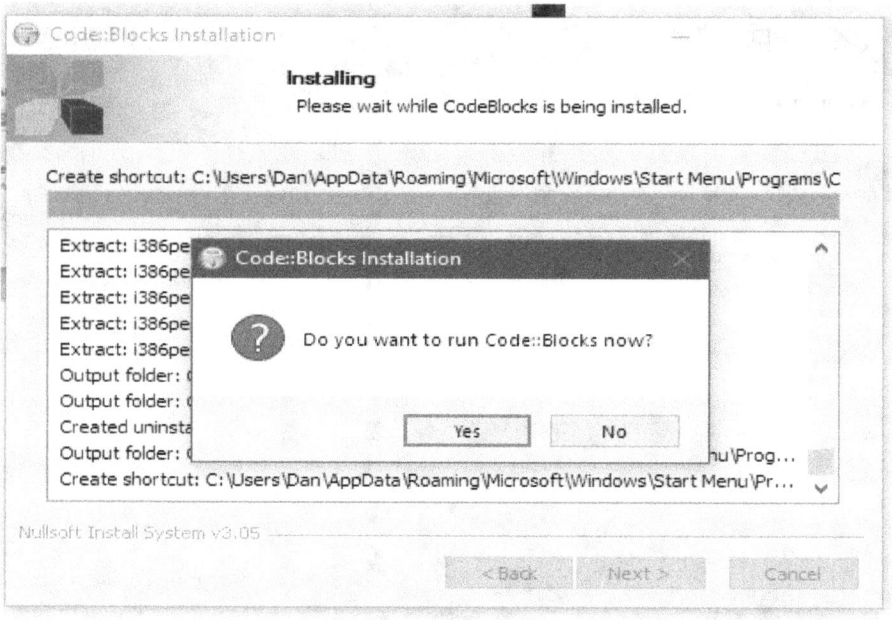

1.3 **Using Code::Blocks**

i.   After installing the application, click file > New > Projects

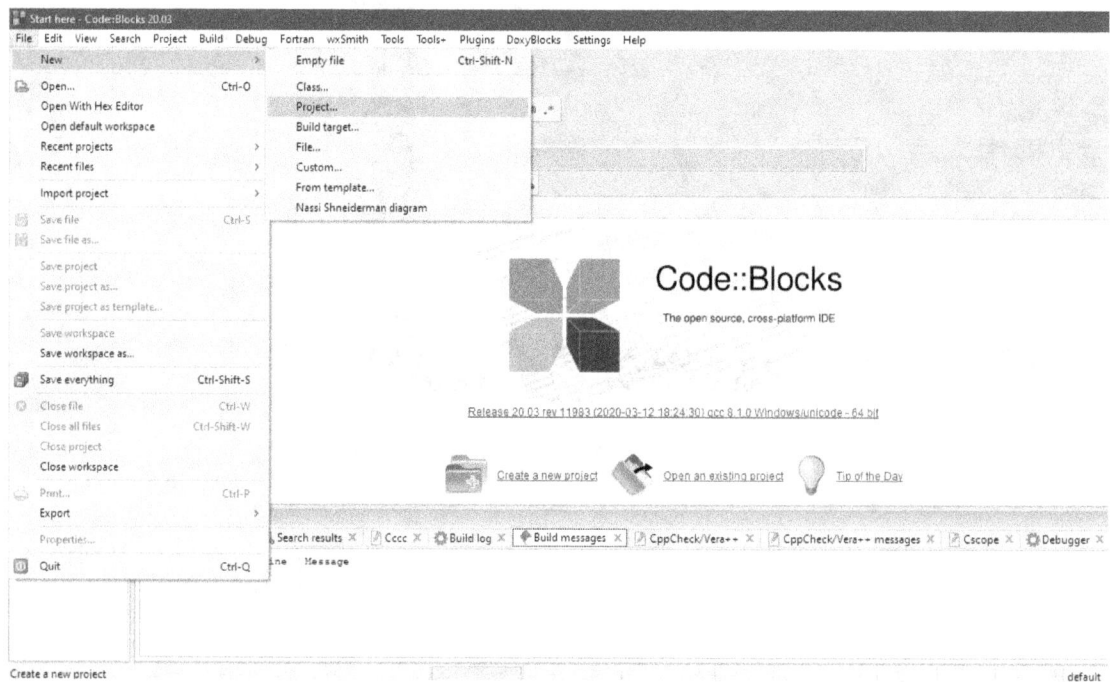

ii.   Select Console Application and click GO

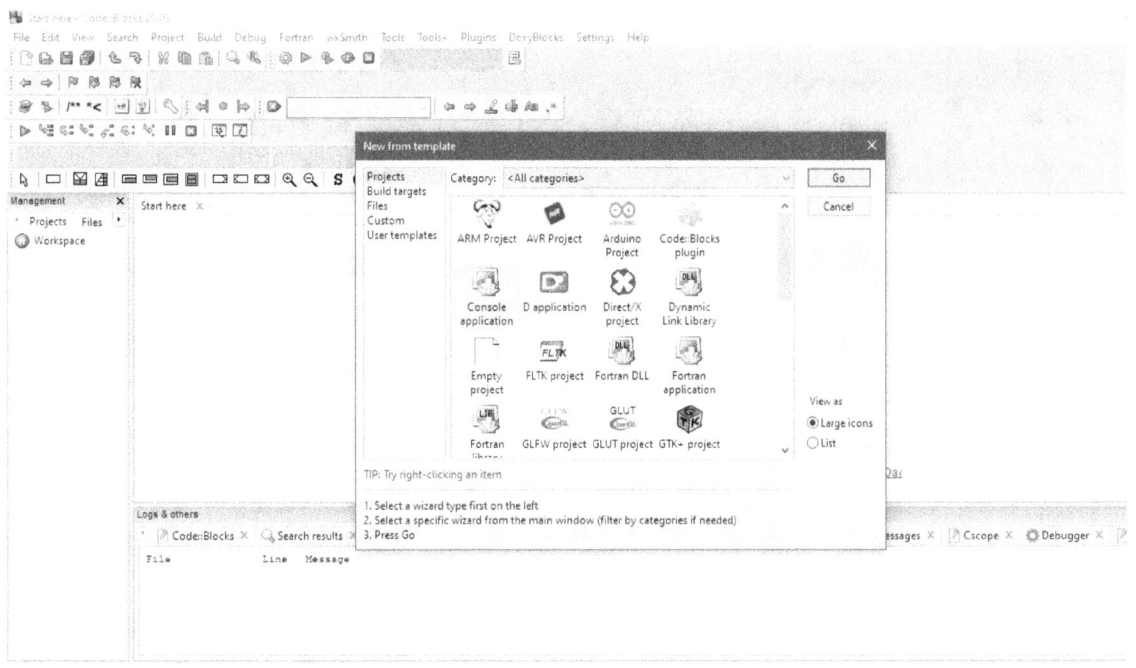

iii. Click Next

iv. Select C++. Click Next.

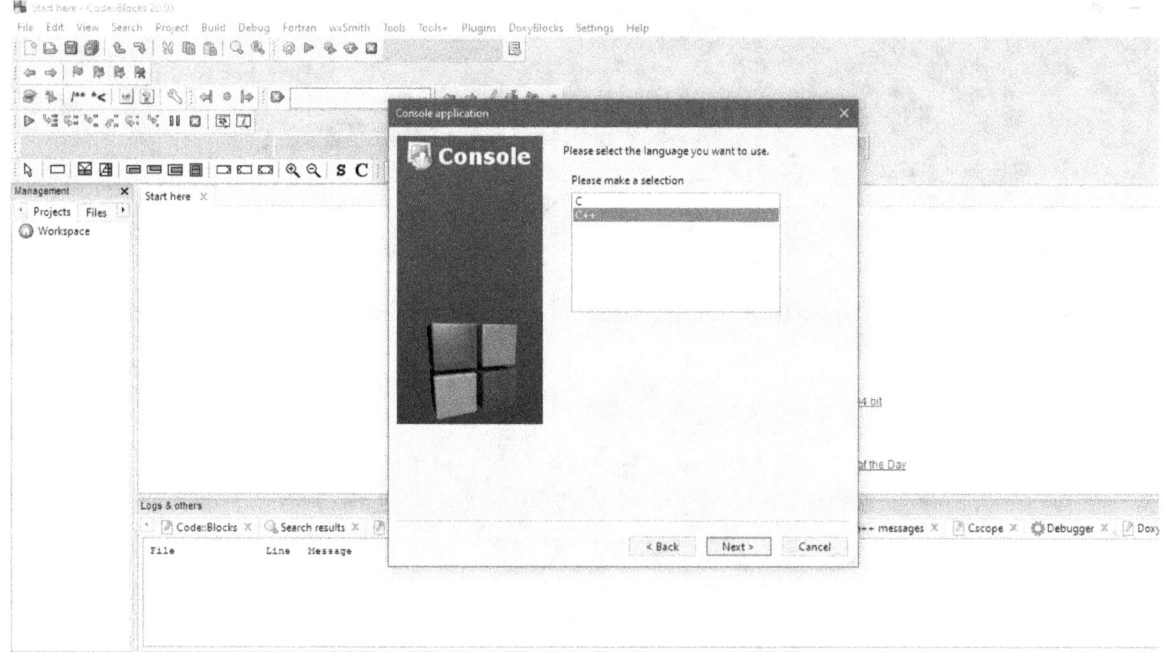

v.   Type a project title and select a folder.

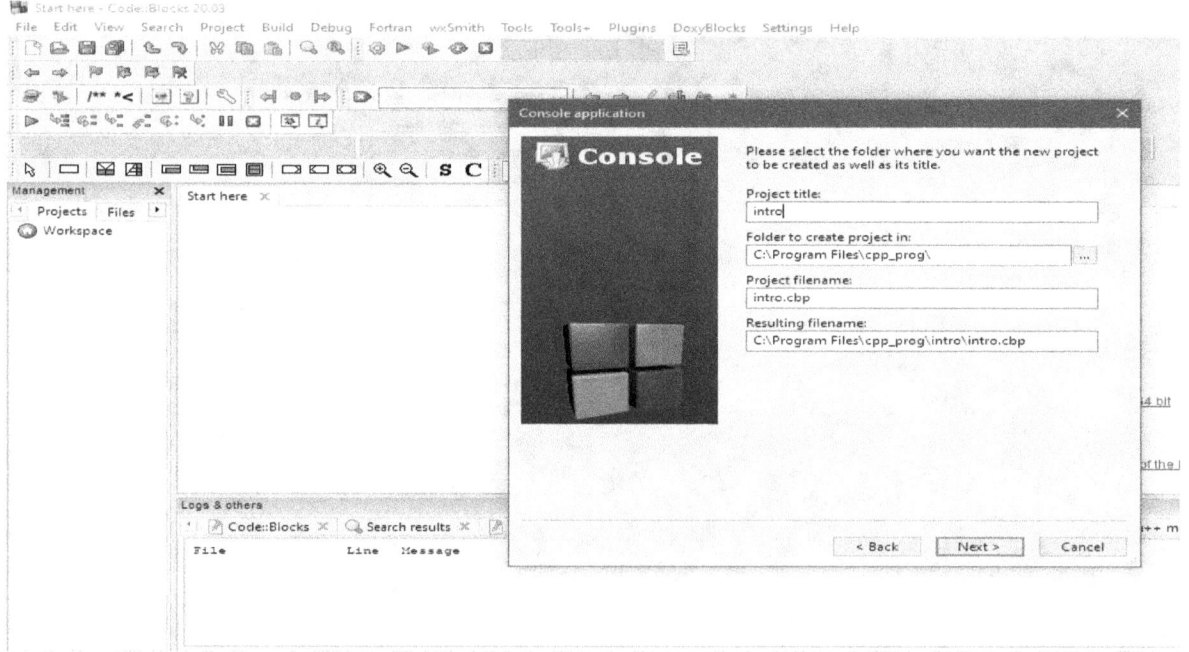

vi.   Make sure the compiler is GNU GCC Compiler. Click Finish.

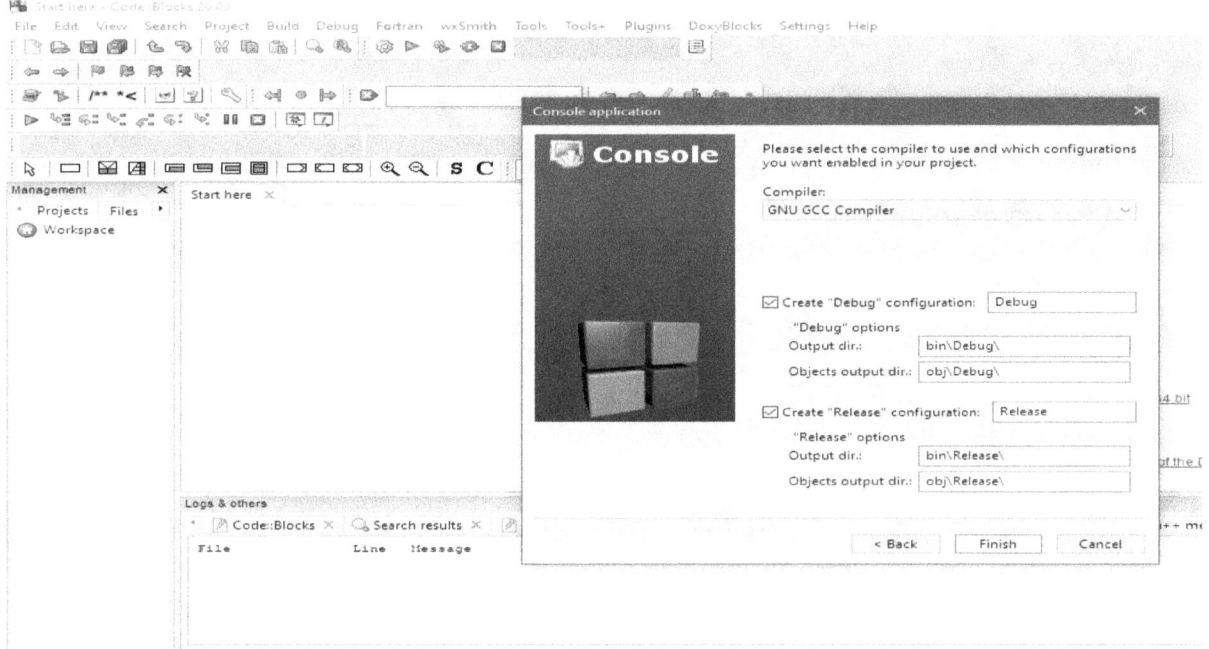

vii.   Click the + sign beside Sources. Click main.cpp.

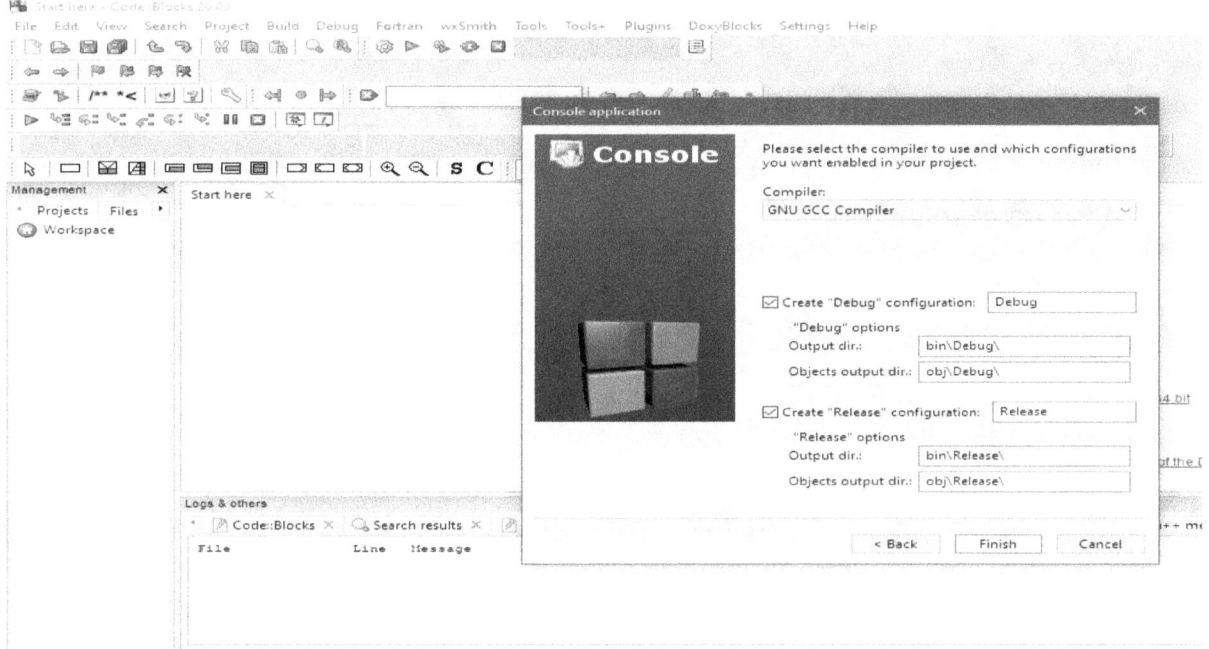

1.4 Writing and running your first C++ program

```cpp
#include <iostream>

using namespace std;

int main()
{

    cout << "I'm learning C++" << endl;

    return 0;

}
```

Figure 1-1

Click *build and run (under wxSmith menu item)*.

```
"C:\Users\Mr. Okwu\Documents\cpp_rev\intro_first\bin\Debug\intro_first.exe"
I'm learning C++

Process returned 0 (0x0)   execution time : 0.038 s
Press any key to continue.
```

Press any key to continue.

Example (fig. -1) explained

The only line of the code you should understand for now is 7 (*cout << "I'm learning C++" << endl;*). The rest will be explained later in the book. *cout* or console output is used for printing to the screen. << is called insertion operator and is associated with *cout*. "I'm learning C++" is a string (a collection of characters) that is displayed when the program is executed. *endl* is for new line (like Enter on a keyboard). It can be replaced by \n. In this statement, *endl* is not necessary because there only one statement. Every C++ statement ends with semi-colon.

Exercise

1. Write a C++ program that displays "C++ is a high-level programming language."

Chapter 2: Data Types and Variables

2.1 Data Types in C++

A data type is a classification of data which tells a compiler or interpreter the type of value assigned to a variable and the types of operations that can be carried out on it.

The following data types are assigned to variables in C++:

i. int: A whole number such as 3 and 197.

ii. string: A collection of characters enclosed in quotes.

iii. float: A number with decimal point correct to six decimal places.

iv. double: A number with a decimal point correct to ten decimal places

v. bool: A Boolean value of true or false.

vi. char: A single character enclosed in single quotes.

2.2 Variables

A variable is a named memory location which holds a value. In this context, it is a container that holds a value. The container is given a name for referencing the content of the container. The content of the variable can change.

The following rules must be observed in giving names to variables:

i. Names of variables must start with letters or underscores.

ii.   Names of variables are case sensitive (myName and MyName are different variables.

iii.   Whitespaces are not allowed in names of variables.

iv.   Special characters such as #, %, !, et cetera are not allowed

v.   Reserved keywords in C++ (e. g. int, while, class, etc.) as not allowed

Variables must be declared before they can be used in C++ programs. The syntax for creating or declaring variable is as follows:

Datatype nameOfVariable = value;

If you do not want the value of a variable to change, use the keyword *const* to declare it. For example, *const secondsPerMinute = 60;*

Example 2-1

```cpp
#include <iostream>
using namespace std;
int main()
{
    // Declare variables
    int num1 = 7;
    float num2 = 9.81;
    double num3 = 3.1428571;
    string myName = "Dan";
    char grade = 'A';
    bool isTall = true;
    /*
    This is a multi-line comment
    Print of display the value of each variable
    */
    cout << num1 << endl;
    cout << num2 << "\n";
    cout << num3 << "\n";
    cout << myName << "\n";
    cout << grade << "\n";
    cout << isTall;
    return 0;
}
```

```cpp
#include <iostream>

using namespace std;

int main()
{
    // Declare variables
    int num1 = 7;
    float num2 = 9.81;
    double num3 = 3.1428571;
    string myName = "Dan";
    char grade = 'A';
    bool isTall = true;

    /* This is a multi-line comment
    Print to display the value of each variable.
    */

    cout << num1 << "\n";
    cout << num2 << "\n";
    cout << num3 << "\n";
    cout << myName << "\n";
    cout << grade << "\n";
    cout << isTall;

    return 0;
}
```

```
7
9.81
3.14286
Dan
A
1
Process returned 0 (0x0)    execution time : 0.103 s
Press any key to continue.
```

Output of example 2-1

Example 2-1 Explained

In line 7, there is a single line comment. Comments are used to clarify statements in a code. They are ignored by the compiler. A multi-line comment is included in lines 15 through 18.

In lines 8 through 13, variables of different types are declared and initialized (assigned values).

In line 19 through 24, instructions for printing the values of the variables are given.

In the output the value of *isTall* is 1. True has the numerical value of 1 while false is 0.

2.3 Exercises

i. Declare a variable named age, assign a value to it and execute the program to display the value on the screen

ii. Create a variable named weight, assign a value to it and execute the program to print the value to the screen.

Chapter 3: Input / Output

Accepting inputs and producing outputs are some of the basic operations of computers. The others are processing and storing data.

As we have seen already, *cout* is used for outputting values. *cin* is used for accepting values. When using cin, words with a space are truncated. For example, if you enter *learning programming*, only *learning* will be accepted. To get the computer to accept the two words, a function, *getline(cin, phrase)*, is used. Function will be explained in a later chapter.

Example 3-1

```cpp
#include <iostream>
using namespace std;
int main()
{
    // Declare variables but do not initialize them
    int firstNumber;
    int secondNumber, sum;

    // Display instructions for users
    cout << "Enter the first number \n";
    cin >> firstNumber;
    cout << "Enter another number \n";
    cin >> secondNumber;

    sum = firstNumber + secondNumber;

    cout << "The sum is " << sum;
    return 0;
}
```

```cpp
#include <iostream>

using namespace std;

int main()
{
    // Declare variables but do not initialize them
    int firstNumber;
    int secondNumber, sum;

    // Display instruction for users
    cout << "Enter the first number \n";
    cin >> firstNumber;

    cout << "Enter another number \n";
    cin >> secondNumber;

    sum = firstNumber + secondNumber;

    cout <<"The sum is " << sum;

    return 0;
}
```

Output of example 3-1

```
Enter the first number
65
Enter another number
30
The sum is 95
Process returned 0 (0x0)    execution time : 6.523 s
Press any key to continue.
```

Example 3-1 Explained

In lines 8 and 9, variables are declared but values are not assigned to them (not initialized). Note that in line 9, two variables, secondNumber and sum are declared in one statement.

cin (associated with the extraction operator, >>) is used to accept inputs. The values inputted by a user are assigned to firstNumber and secondNumber. The values are added and assigned to the variable *sum.* The assignment operator (=) is used to assign the value on the right to the variable on the left.

cout <<"The sum is " << sum; This line (21) is used to print the content of the variable sum.

Example 3-2

```
#include <iostream>
using namespace std;
int main()
{
    string myName;
    cout << "Type your name \n";
    cin >> myName;
    cout << "Your name is " << myName;
    return 0;
}
```

```cpp
#include <iostream>

using namespace std;

int main()
{
    string myName;
    cout << "Type your name \n";
    cin >> myName;
    cout << "Your name is " << myName;
    return 0;
}
```

Output

```
Type your name
Mr Dan
Your name is Mr
Process returned 0 (0x0)    execution time : 13.807 s
Press any key to continue.
```

Example 3-2 Explained

Line 7: *string myName;*

A variable named myName is created with a data type of string.

Line 9: *cin >> myName;*

This statement is used for accepting the value entered by a user. The value is stored in myName.

In the output, I typed Mr Dan but only Mr was displayed on the screen. As stated earlier, to display multiple values, the function getline() is used. This is demonstrated in the example below.

Example 3-3

```cpp
#include <iostream>

using namespace std;

int main()
{
    string myName;
    cout << "Type your name \n";
    getline(cin, myName);
    cout << "Your name is " << myName;
    return 0;
}
```

Output of example 3-3

```
"C:\Users\Mr. Okwu\Documents\cpp_rev\var_pro\input_string\bin\Debug\input_string.exe"          —     □
Type your name
Mr Dan
Your name is Mr Dan
Process returned 0 (0x0)   execution time : 7.736 s
Press any key to continue.
```

3.1 Exercises

i. Write a program that accepts two values, adds them and displays the result.

ii. Write a program that accepts and displays two or more words.

Chapter 4: C++ Operators

Operators are used to perform operations on operands (values and variables.

Operators are classified into arithmetic operators, assignment operators, comparison operators and logical operators.

4.1 Arithmetic operators

They include mathematical operators such as addition (+), subtraction (-), multiplication (*), division (/), modulus (%), increment (++) and decrement (--).

Example 4-1

```cpp
#include <iostream>
using namespace std;
int main()
{
    // Declare variables
    int num1 = 2;
    int num2 = 4;
    string greet = "Hello ";
    cout << "Addition " <<num1 + num2 << endl;
    cout << "Subtraction " <<num2 - num1 << endl;
    cout << "Multiplication " <<num2 * num1 << endl;
    cout << "Division " <<num2 / num1 << endl;
    cout << "Remainder " <<5 % num1 << endl;
    cout << "Increment " <<++num1 << endl;
    cout << "Decrement " <<--num1 << endl;
    cout << greet + "Tim" << endl;
    return 0;
}
```

```cpp
#include <iostream>

using namespace std;

int main()
{
    // Declare variables
    int num1 = 2;
    int num2 = 4;
    string greet = "Hello ";

    cout << "Addition: " << num1 + num2 << endl;
    cout << "Subtraction: " << num2 - num1 << endl;
    cout << "Multiplication: " << num1 * num2 << "\n";
    cout << "Division: " << num2 / num1 << endl;
    cout << "Remainder: " << 5 % num1 << endl;
    cout << "Increment: " << ++num1 << endl;
    cout << "Decrement: " << --num1 << endl;
    cout << greet + "Tim" << endl;
    return 0;
}
```

```
Addition: 6
Subtraction: 2
Multiplication: 8
Division: 2
Remainder: 1
Increment: 3
Decrement: 2
Hello Tim

Process returned 0 (0x0)   execution time : 0.025 s
Press any key to continue.
```

Example 4-1 Explained

Most of the arithmetic operators are used in C++and other programming languages the same they are used in elementary mathematics.

cout << "Remainder: " << 5 % num1 << endl; This statement in line 16 uses the modulus operator to find the remainder after division.

cout << "Increment: " << ++num1 << endl; In line 17, the increment operator which increases a number by 1 before outputting it is used. This is a case of pre-increment. There is also post-increment in which the number is outputted before being increased. The post-increment form is expressed as num1++.

In line 19 (*cout << greet + "Tim" << endl;*), the same operator used for adding numbers is used to combine strings. This is known as concatenation.

4.2 Assignment operators

An assignment operator is used to assign a value to a variable. For example, *int num = 3;*

The assignment operator, =, can be combined with arithmetic operators as shown below:

int num1 = 4;

num1 += 7

This means num1 = num1 + 7. The answer is 11. Other arithmetic operators can be combined with the assignment operator in the same way.

4.3 Comparison Operators

They are used to compare two values or variables. The result of the comparison is either true or false.

Examples of comparison operators include:

Operator	Name
>	Greater than
<	Less than
>=	Greater than or equal to
<=	Less than or equal to
==	Equal to
!=	Not equal to

We will use these operators in later chapters, especially in decision-making.

4.4 Logical Operators

Like comparison operators, the result of comparing values or variables using logical operators must be true or false.

Examples of logical operators

Operator	Name	Usage
&&	Logical and	Both conditions must be true for true to be returned.
||	Logical or	True is returned if one of the conditions is true.
!	Logical not	Negation of a condition. Not true means false.

We will use logical operators in our code in later chapters.

4.5 Exercise

i. Write a C++ program to divide a number by another number and print the remainder.

ii. Use the subtraction assignment operator to subtract the value 3 from a variable y.

iii. Write a program that accepts 5 marks in five subjects. Calculate the total, average and print them to the console.

Chapter 5: Making Decisions

One of the reasons computers were invented is to automate boring and repetitive tasks. Computers are also good at making decisions. When they make decisions, only one of two options is selected at a time. The comparison and logical operators we saw earlier are used in instructing computers to make decisions.

5.1 If...else statement

This is used to specify a block of code that will be executed if a condition is true and a block of code that will be executed if a conditions is false.

The syntax of *if...else* statement is as follows:

```
if (condition) {

    // execute this block of code if condition is true

} else {

    // execute this block of code if condition is false}
```

Example 5-1a

```
if (9 > 7) {

        cout <<"9 is greater than 7";

} else {

        cout << "The condition is false";

    }
```

Output of example 5-1a

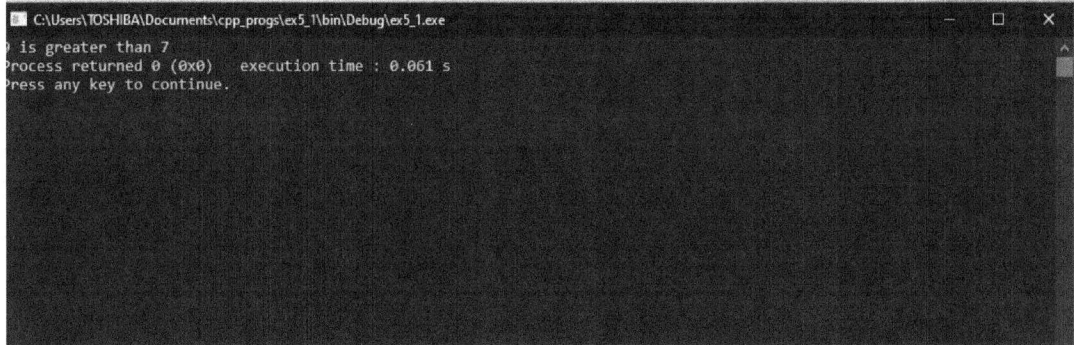

```
C:\Users\TOSHIBA\Documents\cpp_progs\ex5_1\bin\Debug\ex5_1.exe                         —    □    ×
  is greater than 7
Process returned 0 (0x0)    execution time : 0.061 s
Press any key to continue.
```

The syntax for testing two or more conditions is as follows:

if (*condition*) {

   // execute this block of code if condition is true

} else if (*condition*) {

   // execute this block of code if condition is true

} else {

// execute this block of code if none of the conditions is true

}

Example 5-1b: Making a simple calculator

#include <iostream>

using namespace std;

int main(){

// Implement a simple calculator

/*

Multi-line comment

```
Declare variables
*/
float num1, num2, sum, subtr, div, mult;

string entered;

cout <<"Enter a number: \n";

cin >>num1;

cout <<"Enter another number: \n";

cin >>num2;

cout <<"Enter an operator(+, -,/, *): \n";

cin >> entered;

if(entered == "+"){

        sum = num1 + num2;

        cout <<"The sum is: " <<sum <<"\n";

} else if(entered == "-"){

        subtr = num1 - num2;

        cout <<"The difference is: " <<subtr <<endl;

}else if(entered == "/"){

        div = num1 / num2;

        cout <<"The quotient is: " <<div <<endl;

} else if (entered == "*"){
```

```
    mult = num1 * num2;

    cout <<"The product is: " <<mult <<endl;

} else {

    cout <<"Enter the correct operator";

}

return 0;

}
```

Output of example 5-1b

```
"C:\Users\Mr. Okwu\Documents\cpp_rev\var_pro\simple_calc\bin\Debug\simple_calc.exe"
Enter a number:
97
Enter another number:
2
Enter an operator(+, -,/, *):
/
The quotient is: 48.5

Process returned 0 (0x0)   execution time : 11.405 s
Press any key to continue.
```

Example 5-1c: Using AND logical operator

```cpp
#include <iostream>

using namespace std;

int main()

{

    int mathScore = 51; // Declare and initialize variable

    int engScore = 60;


    // Using logical AND operator

    if ((mathScore >= 50) && (engScore >= 50)) {

        cout << "Passed" << endl;

    } else {

        // This block will not be executed because the condition is not false

        cout << "Failed" << endl;

    }

    return 0;

}
```

Output of example 5-1c

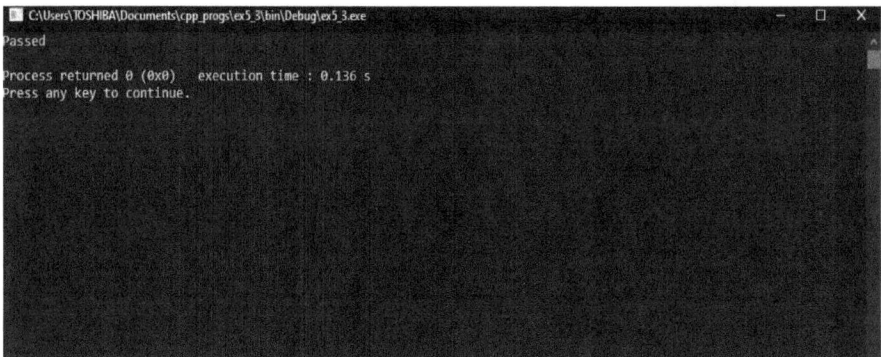

If you change the conditional statement such that mathScore < 50 and engScore >= 60, the else block will be executed. When using the AND operator both conditions must be true.

Example 5-1d: Using OR logical operator

```
#include <iostream>
using namespace std;
int main()
{
    int mathScore = 51; // Declare and initialize variable
    int engScore = 60;
    // Using logical OR operator
    if ((mathScore < 50) || (engScore >= 60)) {
        cout << "Passed" << endl;
    } else {
        // This block will not be executed because the condition is not false
        cout << "Failed" << endl;
    }
    return 0;
}
```

Output of example 5-1d

Passed is displayed because one of the conditions is true. If both conditions are true, the first block (*passed*) is also executed.

5.2 Switch Statements

You can use switch statements in place of a chain of *if—else* statements. Like the *if—else* statement, a block of code is executed when a match is found.

Switch statements are compact and easier to understand compared to a chain of if—else statements.

The syntax of switch statements is as follows:

Switch (expression) {

    case a:

      // block of code

      break;

    case b:

      //block of code

      break;

default:

// block of code

}

After evaluating the expression, the result is compared with each case. The block of code that matches the result of the value of the expression is executed. The break keyword stops the execution of the code as the C++ compiler breaks out of the switch block and stop testing. If no case match is found, the code after the default keyword is executed.

Example 5-2a

```
#include <iostream>

using namespace std;

int main()
{
    int age = 8;
    switch (age) {
    case 4:
        cout <<"pre-school";
        break;
    case 6:
        cout <<"year one pupil";
        break;
    case 7:
        cout <<"year two pupil";
        break;
    case 8:
        cout <<"year 8 student";
        break;
    default:
        cout <<"No match found";
    }
    cout << endl;
    return 0;
}
```

Output of example 5-2a

```
"C:\Users\Mr. Okwu\Documents\cpp_rev\var_pro\switch\bin\Debug\switch.exe"
year 8 student

Process returned 0 (0x0)    execution time : 0.044 s
Press any key to continue.
```

5.3 Exercises

i. Write a C++ program for determining those who will vote and those who will not vote in an election. Users should be prompted to enter ages of voters. Only those who are 18 and above are eligible to vote. Those who do not meet this criterion should be asked to try next year.

ii. Write a program for determining whether a number is odd or even.

Chapter 6: Loop

Computers excel at doing the same thing over and over. Unlike humans, they are immune to boredom.

A loop allows us to instruct a computer to perform a task many times. A computer performs the specified task until the condition stated in the instruction evaluates to false. In this chapter, you will learn how to use *while loop* and *for loop*.

6.1 *for loop*

The syntax of a *for loop* is as follows:

for (*declare and initialize variable*; *condition*; *increment or decrement*) {

    block of code to execute;

}

The increment / decrement is important to prevent infinite loop.

Example 6-1

```cpp
#include <iostream>

using namespace std;

int main()
{
    for (int i = 0; i < 10; i++){
        cout << i <<" I'm learning for loop" << endl;
    }

    return 0;
}
```

Output of example 6-1

```
0 I'm learning for loop
1 I'm learning for loop
2 I'm learning for loop
3 I'm learning for loop
4 I'm learning for loop
5 I'm learning for loop
6 I'm learning for loop
7 I'm learning for loop
8 I'm learning for loop
9 I'm learning for loop

Process returned 0 (0x0)   execution time : 0.066 s
Press any key to continue.
```

Example 6-1 Explained

```
for (int i = 0; i < 10; i++){

        cout << i <<" I'm learning for loop" << endl;}
```

A variable i is declared given an initial value of 0. The computer checks the condition; it evaluates to true because 0 is less than 10. It prints the statement "I'm learning for loop." It increases *i* by 1 and checks the condition again. It continues to do this until *i* is 10; at this point the condition is false, the loop ends.

6.2 *while loop*

While the syntax for *while loop* is different from the syntax for *for loop*, they do the same thing—repeat a statement many times until the condition is false.

Syntax

Declare variable

while (condition){

```
// Block of code to run

    update

}
```

Example 6-2

Output of Example 6-2

6.3 Exercises

i. Write a program to display odd numbers between 0 and 40.

ii. Write a program that counts from 10 to 1.

Chapter 7: Functions

7.1 What is a function?

A function is a block of code which can be called to perform a task. A function helps us reduce repetition of code since it can be defined once and called many times. You can pass data into a function when it is called.

7.2 Creating C++ Functions

The syntax for creating or declaring C++ functions is as follows:

return type nameOfFunction() {

    //code to be executed

}

If the function does not have a return value, it is created as follows:

void functionName() {

    // code to be executed

}

Example 7-2a

Project   Build   Debug   Fortran   wxSmith   Tools   Tools+   Plugins   DoxyBlocks   Settings   Help

main.cpp ✕   main.cpp ✕   main.cpp ✕   main.cpp ✕   main.cpp ✕   main.cpp ✕   main.cpp ✕

```cpp
1        #include <iostream>
2
3        using namespace std;
4
5        void greeting () { // Declaration of function
6            // Definition of function
7            string herName = "Jane";
8            cout << "Good morning " + herName;
9        }
10
11       int main()
12       {
13           // call the function
14           greeting() ;
15           return 0;
16       }
```

Example 7-2a Explained

On line 5, the function is declared. This function does not have a returned value since it is declared with keyword "void".

Function definition begins on line 6. This means writing the code or statements that will be executed in the body of the function.

On line 14, the function is called. This means typing or writing the name of the function followed by parenthesis. It can be called many times.

Example 7-2c

```
roject  Build  Debug  Fortran  wxSmith  Tools  Tools+  Plugins  DoxyBlocks  Settings  Help

                  square(int s) : int

main.cpp ×  main.cpp ×  main.cpp ×  main.cpp ×  main.cpp ×  main.cpp ×  main.cpp ×  main.cpp ×
      1        #include <iostream>
      2
      3        using namespace std;
      4
      5      int square ( int s ) {
      6            return s * s;
      7      }
      8
      9      int main()
     10     {
     11          int num;
     12          cout << "Enter a number ";
     13          cin >> num;
     14          // call the function
     15          cout << square(num) << endl;
     16          return 0;
     17     }
     18
```

Example 7-2c Explained

On line 5, a function with a return type of *int* is declared. This function has a parameter (the variable s inside the parentheses). When we call the function, we must pass data (argument) into it.

On line 6, the return keyword is used because this function returns a value to the caller. The value can be assigned to a variable and used later.

When the function is called on line 15, the data entered by a user is passed into it; this is called an argument.

Example 7-2d: A function with multiple parameters

```cpp
1    #include <iostream>
2
3    using namespace std;
4
5    float rectangle ( float width, float lengthRec ) {
6        return width * lengthRec;
7    }
8
9    int main()
10   {
11       float num1;
12       float num2;
13       cout << "Enter a width: ";
14       cin >> num1;
15       cout << "Enter a length: ";
16       cin >> num2;
17       // call the function
18       float result = rectangle(num1, num2);
19       cout << "The area: "<< result <<endl;
20       return 0;
21   }
22
```

Example 7-2d Explained

On line 5, a function named rectangle with a return type of float is created. It has two parameters.

On lines 14 and 16, the program receives data from user and the values are assigned to variables *num1* and *num2*.

The function is called on line 18 and given num1 and num2 as arguments. The value is assigned to a variable (*result*). The value of result is printed to the console on line 19.

7.3 Built-in Math Functions

The example below shows how some built-in C++ functions are used in performing mathematical operations on numbers.

Example 7-3a

```
de::Blocks 20.03
roject  Build  Debug  Fortran  wxSmith  Tools  Tools+  Plugins  DoxyBlocks  Settings  Help
```

```
main() : int
```

```
main.cpp  main.cpp  main.cpp  main.cpp  main.cpp  main.cpp  main.cpp  main.cpp  main.cpp  main.cpp
     1     #include <iostream>
     2
     3     using namespace std;
     4
     5     int main()
     6     {
     7
     8         cout << "The highest value " << max(7, 2)<< endl; // find the highest value of the two numbers
     9         cout <<"The lowest value " << min(9, 3) << endl; // find the highest value of the two numbers
    10         return 0;
    11     }
    12
```

Output of example 7-3a

```
Select "C:\Users\Mr. Okwu\Documents\cpp_rev\var_pro\math_func\bin\Debug\math_func.exe"
The highest value 7
The lowest value 3

Process returned 0 (0x0)   execution time : 0.047 s
Press any key to continue.
```

Example 7-3b: Using other functions in C++ <cmath> header

main.cpp × main.cpp × main.cpp × main.cpp × main.cpp × main.cpp × main.cpp × main.cpp × main.cpp × main.cpp ×

```cpp
1      #include <iostream>
2
3      using namespace std;
4      #include <cmath>
5
6      int main()
7      {
8
9          cout << pow(7, 2) << endl; // 7 raised to the power of 2
10         cout  << sqrt(9) << endl; // square root of 9
11         cout << round(8.27) << "\n";
12         cout << floor(3.5) << "\n";
13         cout << ceil(3.5) << "\n";
14         return 0;
15     }
16
```

Logs & others

Code::Blocks ×   Search results ×   Cccc ×   Build log ×   Build messages ×   CppCheck/Vera++ ×   CppCheck/Vera++ messa

Output of 7-3b

```
Select "C:\Users\Mr. Okwu\Documents\cpp_rev\var_pro\math_func\bin\Debug\math_func.exe"
49
3
8
3
4

Process returned 0 (0x0)   execution time : 0.063 s
Press any key to continue.
```

7.4 Recursive functions

A recursive function is a function that calls itself. The technique for making a function to call itself is known as recursion.

When properly written, recursion is an elegant solution to some problems as it breaks down the problem into small parts that can be easily solved. On the other hand, it can use too much memory or lead to infinite loop. To prevent infinite loop, there should be a base case to bring the recursion to an end.

Calculating the factorial of a number will be used to demonstrate how to write a recursive function. The factorial of a number, n, is the product of n and all the numbers less than n but greater than 0. Note that the factorial of 0 and 1 is 1. This is taken into account in example 7-4. The factorial of 6 (6!) is 1 * 2 * 3 * 4 * 5 * 6 = 720.

Example 7-4

```cpp
1    #include <iostream>
2
3    using namespace std;
4    int factorial(int n) {
5        if ((n==0) || (n==1)) {
6            return 1;
7        } else {
8            return n * factorial(n-1);
9        }
10   }
11
12   int main()
13   {
14       int n;
15       cout << "Enter an integer " << endl;
16       cin >> n;
17       cout << "The factorial of " << n << " is " << factorial(n);
18       return 0;
19   }
20
```

Logs & others

```
"C:\Users\Mr. Okwu\Documents\cpp_rev\var_pro\fact\bin\Debug\fact.exe"
Enter an integer
6
The factorial of 6 is 720
Process returned 0 (0x0)     execution time : 1.968 s
Press any key to continue.
```

Example 7-4 Explained

A function called factorial is declared as follows:

int factorial(int n) {

   if ((n==0) || (n==1)) {

     return 1;

   } else {

     return n * factorial(n-1);

   }

}

The function takes a parameter n. If the value of n equals 0 or 1, 1 is returned. As stated earlier, the factorial of 0 and 1 is 1. These serve as the base cases in the code snippet above. If the value of is not equal to 0 or 1, the function calls itself in *n * factorial(n - 1)* and the result is returned to the caller.

The function is called in the *main* function after a user has entered a number

7.5 Exercises

i.   Create a function that accepts a name when it is called and uses the name in a greeting.

ii.   Write a program that uses a function in calculating the area of a triangle.

iii.   Write a function that uses a function to calculate the average of three numbers

Chapter 8: Arrays

An array is a special type of variable that stores multiple values in one variable.

8.1 Creating an array and accessing the elements of an array

The syntax for creating an array is as follows:

variable type nameOfArray [number of elements]

An array that stores 5 numbers can be created as follows:

int numbers[5] = {7, 1, 44, 3, 9}

Arrays are zero-indexed. Using the example above, the first element, 7, is at index position 0, 1 is t index position 2 and so on.

Example 8-1

```cpp
#include <iostream>

using namespace std;

int main()
{
    // Create an array
    string students [4] = {"John", "Peter", "Austin", "Obi"};

    //Access elements of the array
    cout << students[0] << endl;
    cout << students[3] << endl;


    // Change an element of the array
    students[3] = "Jane";
    cout << students[3] << endl;
    return 0;
}
```

Output of example 8-1

```
"C:\Users\Mr. Okwu\Documents\cpp_rev\var_pro\array1\bin\Debug\array1.exe"
John
Obi
Jane

Process returned 0 (0x0)    execution time : 0.066 s
Press any key to continue.
```

Example 8-1 Explained

On line 7, the statement *string students [4] = {"John", "Peter", "Austin", "Obi"};* is used to declare an array of type string with four elements.

On lines 11 and 12, the *statements cout << students[0] << endl;* and *cout << students[3] << endl;* are used to access the first and fourth elements of the array respectively.

On line 16, *students[3] = "Jane";* is used to change the fourth element from Obi to Jane.

8.2 Looping through an array

If you know the number of elements in an array, you can use a *for* loop to access all the elements of the array.

The following examples demonstrate how to loop through the elements of arrays.

Example 8-2a

roject Build Debug Fortran wxSmith Tools Tools+ Plugins DoxyBlocks Settings Help

main() : int

main.cpp × main.cpp × main.cpp × main.cpp × main.cpp × main.cpp × main.cpp × main.cpp × main.cpp >

```cpp
1     #include <iostream>
2
3     using namespace std;
4
5     int main()
6     {
7         // Create an array
8         string students [4] = {"John", "Peter", "Austin", "Obi"};
9
10        // Loop through the array
11        for(int i = 0; i < 4; i++){
12            cout << students[i] << "\n";
13        }
14        return 0;
15    }
16
```

Logs & others

Output of example 8-2a

"C:\Users\Mr. Okwu\Documents\cpp_rev\var_pro\array1\bin\Debug\array1.exe"

```
John
Peter
Austin
Obi

Process returned -1073741819 (0xC0000005)    execution time : 1.469 s
Press any key to continue.
```

Example 8-2a Explained

There are four iterations, 0, 1, 2 and 3. An iteration is a single execution of a set of instructions that are to be repeated. During the first iteration, i, with an initial value of 0 is assigned the element with index 0 (John) after ensuring that the condition is true. 1 is added to i (0 + 1), the condition (i < 4) evaluates to true, and thus the element with index 1 (Peter) is assigned to i and outputted. This continues until all the elements are assigned to i and the condition evaluates to false.

If you do not know the number of elements in an array, a *for* loop can be used but you have to find the size of the array dynamically.

Example 8-2b demonstrates how to find the size of an array.

Example 8-2b

Output of 8-2b

```
"C:\Users\Mr. Okwu\Documents\cpp_rev\var_pro\array1\bin\Debug\array1.exe"
16
Number of elements: 4
Process returned 0 (0x0)    execution time : 0.047 s
Press any key to continue.
```

Why do we have 16 in the output? The *sizeof()* operator returns the size of a data type in bytes. 4 bytes are used to store integer values in memory. Since there are 4 elements in the array, it takes 4 * 4 bytes of space. In order to determine the number of elements in the array, sizeof(numbers) is divided by sizeof(int).

The above explanation will be applied in the following example in looping through an array using a *for* loop. The advantage of this is that you do not have to specify the size of an array; it works for arrays of all sizes.

Example 8-2c

```
ject  Build  Debug  Fortran  wxSmith  Tools  Tools+  Plugins  DoxyBlocks  Settings  Help
                                      main() : int

main.cpp ×  main.cpp ×  main.cpp ×  main.cpp ×  main.cpp ×  main.cpp ×  main.cpp ×  main.cpp ×  main.cpp ×
     1        #include <iostream>
     2
     3     using namespace std;
     4
     5     int main()
     6     {
     7        // Create an array
     8        int numbers[4] = {9, 7, 3, 4};
     9
    10        for(int i = 0; i < sizeof(numbers) / sizeof(int); i++) {
    11           cout << numbers[i] << "\n";
    12        }
    13
    14        return 0;
    15     }
    16
```

Logs & others

Code::Blocks ×   Search results ×   Cccc ×   Build log ×   Build messages ×   CppCheck/Vera++ ×

Output of example 8-2c

"C:\Users\Mr. Okwu\Documents\cpp_rev\var_pro\array1\bin\Debug\array1.exe"

```
9
7
3
4

Process returned 0 (0x0)   execution time : 0.065 s
Press any key to continue.
```

Example 8-2d: Looping through an array using *for each* loop

The results are the same but the syntax is relatively simpler.

```
#include <iostream>

using namespace std;

int main()
{
    // Create an array
    int numbers[4] = {9, 7, 3, 4};

    for(int i : numbers) {
        cout << i << "\n";
    }

    return 0;
}
```

8.3 Multi-dimensional arrays

A multi-dimensional array is an array of arrays.

The syntax for declaring a multi-dimensional array is as follows:

variable type arrayName[number of elements in the main array][number of elements in the sub-arrays]

Example 8-3a: Two dimensional array

```
Blocks 20.03
Project  Build  Debug  Fortran  wxSmith  Tools  Tools+  Plugins  DoxyBlocks  Settings  Help
                          Debug

          main() : int

main.cpp X  main.cpp X  main.cpp X  main.cpp X  main.cpp X  main.cpp X  main.cpp X  main.cpp X  main.cpp X
     1      #include <iostream>
     2
     3      using namespace std;
     4
     5      int main()
     6    {
     7        // Create a multi-dimensional array
     8        int numbersArrays[2][4] = {
     9          {3, 2, 7, 4},
    10          {5, 6, 8, 9}
    11        };
    12
    13        // Access elements of the array
    14        cout << numbersArrays[0][2] << "\n"; // This outputs 7
    15        cout << numbersArrays[1][3] << "\n"; // This outputs 9
    16
    17
    18        return 0;
    19    }
    20
```

Example 8-3a Explained

In *cout << numbersArrays[0][2] << "\n";* (line 14), 0 represents the first row while 2 represents the third column of numbersArrays.

In cout << numbersArrays[1][3] << "\n" (line 15), 1 represents the second row while 3 represents the fourth column of numbersArrays.

Changing Elements in a Multi-Dimensional Array

Using example 8-3a, 5 can be changed as follows:

```cpp
#include <iostream>

using namespace std;

int main()
{
    // Create a multi-dimensional array
    int numbersArrays[2][4] = {
        {3, 2, 7,4},
        {5, 6, 8, 9}
    };
    numbersArrays[1][0] = 17;
    cout << numbersArrays[1][0] << "\n"; // This outputs 17 instead of 5
    return 0;
}
```

Looping Through a Multi-Dimensional Array

Using a loop for each of an array's dimension, you can print all the elements of an array to the console. This is demonstrated in below:

Example 8-3b

```cpp
#include <iostream>

using namespace std;

int main()
{
    // Create a multi-dimensional array
    int numbersArrays[2][4] = {
        {3, 2, 7,4},
        {5, 6, 8, 9}
    };
    // Looping through a multi-dimensional array
    for (int i = 0; i < 2; i++){
        for (int j = 0; j < 4; j++){
            cout << numbersArrays[i][j] << "\n";
        }
    }
    return 0;
}
```

Output of example 8-3b

```
"C:\Users\Mr. Okwu\Documents\cpp_rev\var_pro\array1\bin\Debug\array1.exe"
3
2
7
4
5
6
8
9

Process returned 0 (0x0)   execution time : 0.109 s
Press any key to continue.
```

8.4 Exercises

1. Create a loop named *cars* with names of six car models as elements. Output the first and fourth elements of the array. Change the fourth element of the array.

2. Write a loop to output all the elements of the *cars* array.

3. Create a multi-dimensional array of type string with two rows and four columns. Write a loop to output all the elements of the loop.

Chapter 9: C++ Structures

9.1 What is a C++ structure?

A C++ structure or *struct* is a way of grouping related variables. In this grouping, each variable is known as a member of the structure.

After reading the definition, you are probably thinking about how this is different from an array. An array is a variable that holds multiple values. A structure has multiple variables. In addition, a structure can have different data types; an array cannot.

9.2 Creating a structure and accessing structure members

The syntax for creating a structure is as follows:

```
struct {

// member variables

} nameOfStructure variable
```

Example 9-2a

```cpp
#include <iostream>

using namespace std;

int main()
{
    struct {
        string name;
        int age;
    }students;

    // Assigning values to the members
    students.name = "Joy";
    students.age = 16;

    // Output members of students
    cout << students.name << endl;
    cout << students.age << endl;
    return 0;
}
```

Output of 9-2a

```
Joy
16

Process returned 0 (0x0)   execution time : 0.047 s
Press any key to continue.
```

One structure can be used in multiple variables. This is shown in the example below.

Example 9-2b

```cpp
5      int main()
6      {
7          struct {
8              string name;
9              int age;
10         }student1, student2;
11
12         // Assigning data to the first structure
13         student1.name = "Jean";
14         student1.age = 17;
15
16         // Assigning data to the second structure
17         student2.name = "Dan";
18         student2.age = 19;
19
20         // Output members of the structure
21         cout << student1.name <<" " <<student1.age << endl;
22         cout << student2.name <<" " <<student2.age << endl;
23         return 0;
24     }
25
```

Output of example 9-2b

```
Jean 17
Dan 19

Process returned 0 (0x0)    execution time : 0.047 s
Press any key to continue.
```

Named Structures

You can turn a structure into a data type by giving it a name. This allows you to create variables with the structure.

The example below shows how to turn a structure into a data type for creating variables.

Example 9-2c

Output of example 9-2c

9.3 Exercise

1. Create a structure named rectangle. Declare two members named length and width, assign values to the members and print members of the structure.

Chapter 10: References

A reference is a variable that points to an existing variable and is assigned the same value as the existing variable. It is created by giving the reference name the prefix of & (operator).

10.1 How to create references

In example 10-1a, a variable named myName is created and assigned the value of "Mr. Dan." A reference variable named fname is also created. Both the existing variable and the reference variable print the same value— Mr. Dan—to the screen.

Example 10-1a

```
ks 20.03
oject  Build  Debug  Fortran  wxSmith  Tools  Tools+  Plugins  DoxyBlocks  Settings  Help

                          main() : int

 main.cpp  ×  main.cpp  ×  main.cpp  ×  main.cpp  ×  main.cpp  ×  main.cpp  ×  main.cpp  ×  main.cp
     1        #include <iostream>
     2
     3        using namespace std;
     4
     5        int main()
     6      {
     7          string myName = "Mr. Dan"; // myName variable
     8          string &fname = myName; // reference to myName
     9          cout << myName << endl;
    10          cout << fname << endl;
    11          return 0;
    12      }
    13

Logs & others
     Code::Blocks  ×    Search results  ×    Cccc  ×    Build log  ×    Build messages  ×    CppChe
```

Output of 10-1a

```
"C:\Users\Mr. Okwu\Documents\cpp_rev\var_pro\ref\bin\Debug\ref.exe"
Mr. Dan
Mr. Dan

Process returned 0 (0x0)    execution time : 0.141 s
Press any key to continue.
```

10.2 Memory Address

The & operator was used to create a reference variable in example 10.1a. It is also used to find the memory address of a variable. The memory address refers to the location where the variable is stored in the memory of the computer.

Values assigned to variables are stored in memory addresses which are assigned to variables. We use & operator to get a memory address.

In example 10-2a, the memory address of fname (in hexadecimal) is extracted using the & operator.

Example 10-2a

```cpp
#include <iostream>

using namespace std;

int main()
{
    string myName = "Mr. Dan"; // myName variable
    string &fname = myName; // reference to myName
    cout << myName << endl;
    cout << fname << endl;

    // the memory address of fname
    cout << &fname << endl;
    return 0;
}
```

Output of 10.2a

```
Mr. Dan
Mr. Dan
0x61fde0

Process returned 0 (0x0)   execution time : 0.063 s
Press any key to continue.
```

Chapter 11: Pointers

A pointer is a variable used for storing the memory address of the value assigned to it. As we saw in chapter 10, the memory address of a variable can be extracted using the & operator. The data type of the pointer must be the same as the data type of the value held in the memory address.

11.1 How to create pointers

In example 11-1a, a pointer, ptr, is created and assigned the memory address of myName (using &myName). A pointer is declared with the asterisk symbol *. The memory address is outputted using &myName. Using ptr, the same memory address is outputted. In this way the pointer, ptr, stores the value of myNames' memory address.

Example 11-1a

```cpp
#include <iostream>

using namespace std;

int main()
{
    string myName = "Mr. Dan"; // myName variable
    // ptr is the pointer variable which stores the memory address of myName
    string* ptr = &myName;

    // the memory address of myName
    cout << &myName << endl;

    //Using the pointer to output the memory address
    cout << ptr << endl;
    return 0;
}
```

Output of example 11-1a

```
Select "C:\Users\Mr. Okwu\Documents\cpp_rev\var_pro\ref\bin\Debug\ref.exe"
0x61fde0
0x61fde0

Process returned 0 (0x0)    execution time : 0.062 s
Press any key to continue.
```

11.2 Dereferencing

C++ dereferencing refers to getting the value of a variable using the *
operator. In other words, prefixing ptr with * gives us the value of a variable.
This is shown in example 11-2 below.

Example 11-2

```cpp
1    #include <iostream>
2
3    using namespace std;
4
5    int main()
6    {
7        string myName = "Mr. Dan"; // myName variable
8        // ptr is the pointer variable which stores the memory address of myName
9        string* ptr = &myName;
10
11       // the memory address of myName
12       cout << &myName << endl;
13
14       //Using the pointer to output the memory address
15       cout << ptr << endl;
16
17       // print the value of myName with the pointer (dereference)
18       cout << *ptr << endl;
19       return 0;
20   }
21
```

Output of example 11-2

```
Ox61fde0
Ox61fde0
Mr. Dan

Process returned 0 (0x0)   execution time : 0.047 s
Press any key to continue.
```

11.3 How to modify pointers

In example 11-3, the value of the pointer is changed. This also changes the value of the original variable.

Example 11-3

```
    oject  Build  Debug  Fortran  wxSmith  Tools  Tools+  Plugins  DoxyBlocks  Settings  Help
```

```
                        ∨  main() : int
```

```
    ◀  main.cpp ✕  main.cpp ✕  main.cpp ✕  main.cpp ✕  main.cpp ✕  main.cpp ✕  main.cpp ✕  main.cpp ✕  main.cpp ✕
```

```cpp
4
5        int main()
6      {
7            string myName = "Mr. Dan"; // myName variable
8            // ptr is the pointer variable which stores the memory address of myName
9            string* ptr  = &myName;
10
11           // the memory address of myName
12           cout << &myName << endl;
13
14           //Using the pointer to output the memory address
15           cout <<  ptr << endl;
16
17            // print the value of myName with the pointer (dereference)
18           cout <<  *ptr << endl;
19
20           // changing the value of the pointer
21           *ptr = "Daniel";
22       |
23           // Print the new value of the pointer
24           cout << *ptr << "\n";
25           cout << myName << "\n"; // Print the value of myName variable
26           return 0;
27       }
28
```

Output of example 11-3

```
Clipboard  ⟨  ...  Font  ...  ⟨  ...  Paragraph  ...  ⟨  ...  Styles  ...  ⟨  Editing  ∧ ■
Select "C:\Users\Mr. Okwu\Documents\cpp_rev\var_pro\ref\bin\Debug\ref.exe"
0x61fde0
0x61fde0
Mr. Dan
Daniel
Daniel

Process returned 0 (0x0)   execution time : 0.046 s
Press any key to continue.
```

Exercise

1. Write a program for adding two numbers using pointers.

2. Concatenate two strings using pointers.

Chapter 12: Introduction to Object-Oriented Programming (OOP)

Object-oriented programming is a way of programming by creating objects which contain both data and functions. The data is expressed as attributes while the functions represent functions. Functions that are created inside classes are called methods.

Objects in programming can be compared to real-life objects in the sense that they have properties or attributes and perform some actions. They interact with other objects.

OOP helps us reduce repetition in code. It allows us to create usable applications. Programs written in adherence to the OOP paradigm are fast.

A related concept in OOP is class. A class is a blueprint or template for creating objects. An object is said to be an instance of a class. A class can also be described as a data type for creating objects.

When objects are created, they get their variables or attributes and functions from the class from which they are created.

The table below provides a good analogy between classes and objects in the real, physical world and classes and objects in programming.

Class	Objects
Vehicles	Cars
Attributes	Trucks
Color	Motorcycles
Value	Bicycles
Tires	

A sub-class can be created from the parent class (vehicles) which inherit the attributes and methods (e.g *void move() {statements}* of the parent class. Inheritance is an importance concept in object-oriented programming.

12.1 Creating classes and objects

The syntax for creating a class is as follows:

```
class Student { // The name of the class is student

    public: // The members can be accessed from outside the class

        int age; //An attribute (member)

        string name; //An attribute (member)

};
```

The keyword *class* is used in creating a class. The keyword *public* is an access specifier. Being public, the attributes (variables declared in a class) and methods (functions inside a class) can be accessed from outside the class. If the access specifier is *private*, the attributes and methods cannot be accessed from outside the class. If the access specifier is *protected*, the attributes and methods can only be accessed from inherited classes.

Example 12-1 shows how to create a class and objects.

```cpp
#include <iostream>
using namespace std;
class Student {
public:
    string name;
    int age;
};

int main()
{
    // creating an objects of Student
    Student student1;
    Student student2;
    // Access and assign values to the attributes
    student1.name = "Dan";
    student1.age = 17;
    student2.name = "Okwu";
    student2.age = 16;

    //Print the values of the attributes
    cout << student1.name << endl;
    cout << student1.age << endl;
    cout << student2.name << endl;
    cout << student2.age << endl;
    return 0;
}
```

Output of example 12-1

```
Dan
17
Okwu
16

Process returned 0 (0x0)   execution time : 0.046 s
Press any key to continue.
```

In example 12-1, two objects were created by stating the name of the class followed by the names of the objects (lines 12 and 13). The attributes of the class were accessed using the dot (.) notation (lines 15 to 18).

12.2 Creating Class Methods

When functions are defined inside a class they are called methods.

Functions can also be defined outside a class; they still qualify as methods.

In other words, methods are functions that belong to a class.

In example 12-2a, a function is defined inside a class.

Example 12-2a: Function/method inside a class

```
2      using namespace std;
3    □ class Student {
4      public:
5         string name;
6         int age;
7         // Method
8    □    void say() {
9             cout << "I'm learning C++ programming" << "\n";
10          }
11   └ };
12
13     int main()
14   □ {
15         // creating an objects of Student
16         Student student1;
17         //Calling the method
18         student1.say();
19         // Access and assign values to the attributes
20         student1.name = "Dan";
21         student1.age = 17;
22
23         //Print the values of the attributes
24         cout << student1.name << endl;
25         cout << student1.age << endl;
26         return 0;
27     }
```

Output of example 12-2

```
"C:\Users\Mr. Okwu\Documents\cpp_rev\var_pro\class_obj\bin\Debug\class_obj.exe"
I'm learning C++ programming
Dan
17

Process returned 0 (0x0)     execution time : 0.062 s
Press any key to continue.
```

Example 12-2b: A function defined outside a class

In order to define a function outside a class, you have to declare the function inside the class and define it outside the class.

In example 12-2b, the function/method is declared inside the class with the statement *int studentAge(int age);* This method has a parameter called age. When the function is called, an argument must be provided. Outside the class the function or method is defined using the scope resolution operator (::). The data type is specified, followed by the name of the class, then the scope resolution operator, and followed by the name of the function. This is seen on line 9 as *int Student::studentAge(int age).*

```
1    #include <iostream>
2    using namespace std;
3    class Student {
4    public:
5        // Declare the function inside the class
6        int studentAge(int age);
7    };
8    // Define the function outside the class
9    int Student::studentAge(int age) {
10       return age;
11   }
12
13   int main()
14   {
15       // creating an objects of Student
16       Student student1;
17
18       // Call the function
19       cout << "I'm a " << student1.studentAge(17) <<"-year-old student." << endl;
20
21       return 0;
22   }
23
```

Output of example 12-2b

```
I'm a 17-year-old student.

Process returned 0 (0x0)    execution time : 0.044 s
Press any key to continue.
```

12.3 Constructors

A constructor is a special method that is called automatically when an instance of a class (object) is created.

A constructor is created by using the same class name. It is always public and does not have a return value. Example 12-3a shows how to create a constructor. A constructor can be used to initialize attributes. In example 12-3, the attributes are initialized with the parameters of the constructor. When the constructor is called arguments are provided.

Example 12-3a

```cpp
#include <iostream>
using namespace std;
class Student {
public:
    string name;
    int age;
    //Create a constructor with parameters
    Student(string n, int i) {
        name = n;
        age = i;
    }
};

int main()
{
    // Create Student objects and call the constructor
    Student student1("Linda", 18);
    Student student2("Dan", 17);

    // Output the values
    cout << student1.name<<" " <<student1.age << endl;
    cout << student2.name<<" " <<student2.age << endl;

    return 0;
}
```

Output of example 12-3a

```
Linda 18
Dan 17

Process returned 0 (0x0)   execution time : 0.121 s
Press any key to continue.
```

Example 12-3b: A constructor without a parameter

The example below includes a constructor that does not take a parameter.

Output of example 12-3b

12.4 Encapsulation

Encapsulation is about hiding data from users. The essence of hiding the data is to secure it from being altered while changing a part of the code. To do this, declare class attributes (variables) as private. This is considered best practice. If the access specifier is not stated, the class variables are by default private. Private attributes cannot be accessed from outside the class unless a public method is created within the class. To modify or read private members, use *get* and *set* methods. In example 12-4a, I demonstrate how to do this.

Example 12-4a

```cpp
#include <iostream>

using namespace std;

class Student {
    // Create a private attribute
    private:
        double fee;

    public:
        //Set method
        void setFee(double f) {
            fee= f;
        }
        // Get method
        double getFee() {
            return fee;
        }
};

int main()
{
    Student student1;
    student1.setFee(100000);
    cout << student1.getFee();
    return 0;
}
```

Output of example 12-4a

```
"C:\Users\Mr. Okwu\Documents\cpp_rev\var_pro\constructor_no_param\bin\Debug\constructor_no_param.exe"
100000
Process returned 0 (0x0)    execution time : 0.047 s
Press any key to continue.
```

Example 12-4a explained

Inside the class, a private member called *fee* with a data type of double is created. Being private, it cannot be read or modified from outside the class.

A public method called setFee is created in the same class. Since it is inside the same class as *fee*, it can access the *fee* variable. The variable *fee* is assigned the value of the setFee parameter.

Using still another public method called getFee, the value of *fee* is returned.

We can read and modify the private member *fee* through the public methods after creating an object of the Student class.

12.5 Inheritance

In C++ and other object-oriented programming languages, one class (child) can inherit the attributes of another class (parent). Inheritance allows us to reuse the members of an existing class, and thus make our code concise.

The class that is inheriting from another uses ":" symbol.

In example 12-5a, the DayStudent class (child) inherits the attributes and methods of the Student class (parent).

Example 12-5a

```cpp
#include <iostream>

using namespace std;
// Parent class
class Student {
public:
    string name = "Dan";
    void read() {
        cout << "I'm reading Practical C++. \n";
    }
};

// Child class
class DayStudent: public Student {
public:
    string city = "Abuja";
};

int main()
{
    DayStudent newStudent;
    newStudent.read();
    cout << newStudent.name << " " <<newStudent.city << endl;
    return 0;
}
```

Output of example 12-5a

```
I'm reading Practical C++.
Dan Abuja

Process returned 0 (0x0)   execution time : 0.047 s
Press any key to continue.
```

Example 12-5b: Using *protected* access specifier

If the access specifier is *protected*, the members of the class can be access in the inherited class only. The variable fee is a protected attribute and as such can only be access in the inherited class DayStudent. This is shown in the example below:

```cpp
#include <iostream>
using namespace std;
// Parent class
class Student {
protected:
    double fee;
};
// Child class
class DayStudent: public Student {
public:
    double tuition;
    void setFee(double f) {
        fee = f;
    }
    double getFee() {
        return fee;
    }
};

int main()
{
    DayStudent newStudent;
    newStudent.setFee(100000);
    newStudent.tuition = 40000;
    cout << "Fee: " << newStudent.getFee() << endl;
    cout << "Tuition: " << newStudent.tuition << endl;
    return 0;
}
```

```
Fee: 100000
Tuition: 40000

Process returned 0 (0x0)   execution time : 0.047 s
Press any key to continue.
```

Chapter 13: Working with files

13.1 Creating and writing to files

To create, read and write to files, the *fstream* library is needed as well as the standard <iostream> header. *ifstream* is used for reading from a file and is part of fstream library.

In example 13-1a, I create a file called greeting.txt and write to it.

```cpp
#include <iostream>
#include <fstream>

using namespace std;

int main()
{
    // Creating and opening a text file
    fstream CreateFile("greeting.txt");

    // Writing to the file
    CreateFile << "Good day. This is Practical C++ for Beginners.";

    // Close the file to free memory space
    CreateFile.close();
    return 0;
}
```

13.2 Reading Files

Example 13-1b

```cpp
#include <iostream>
#include <fstream>
#include <string>

using namespace std;

int main()
{
    // Creating and opening a text file
    ofstream CreateFile("greeting.txt");

    // Writing to the file
    CreateFile << "This is Practical C++ for Beginners.";

    // Close the file to free memory space
    CreateFile.close();

    // fileText is used to print the text file to the screen
    string  fileText;

    // Read from the text file
    ifstream ReadFile("greeting.txt");

    // Read each line with a while loop and getline() function
    while (getline (ReadFile, fileText)) {
        // print the text file to the screen
        cout << fileText;

        cout << endl;
    }
    // Close the file
    ReadFile.close();
    return 0;
}
```

Output of example 13.1b

```
This is Practical C++ for Beginners.

Process returned 0 (0x0)   execution time : 0.016 s
Press any key to continue.
```

Search for "greeting.txt" and open the file with a text editor

Chapter 14: C++ Exceptions

14.1 What is an exception?

An exception is an anomalous or exceptional condition that occurs when a program is executed.

Exception handling is used to change the flow of program execution when a specified error is encountered. Exception handling allows you to anticipate problems or errors that may prevent your code from running normally. A problem can arise during program execution as a result of a mistake by a program or incorrect user input.

Exception handling has three parts, namely, *try, throw and catch*. The try block is for testing your code. If a problem is encountered, an exception is thrown. The catch block handles the error.

14.2 Exception handling

In example 14-2a, I show how to handle an exception using the try, throw and catch blocks.

Example 14-2a

Output of 14-2a

Explanation

In example 14-2a, I tested the code in the try block. When the code is executed, a user is prompted to enter a number. The number is assigned to the age variable. If the age is from 18 to 35, line 12 is executed. If the age is outside the range, an exception is thrown in the form of the age entered. The variable yourAge is used to hold and output the value of age.

The catch block which takes a parameter of type int (this is because age is of type int).

Example 14-2b

Example 14-2a is modified in example 14-2b to handle a situation where we do not know the *throw* type. This can be used to handle any exception by using three dots (…) in the parentheses of the catch block.

```cpp
#include <iostream>

using namespace std;

int main()
{
    try {
        int age;
        cout <<"Enter your age: \n";
        cin >> age;
        if ((age >= 18) && (age <= 35)) {
            cout << "You are a youth.";
        } else {
            throw (400);
        }
    }
    catch (...) {
        cout <<"You are not a youth. \n";
        cout << endl;
    }
    return 0;
}
```